Self-Esteem

Mastering Happiness And Emotional Regulation Through
An Indomitable Mindset, Positive Mental Attitude, And
Heightened Self-Awareness

*(Strategies For Conquering Self-Doubt And Cultivating
Confidence In All Circumstances In A Sequential Manner)*

Kristopher Robles

TABLE OF CONTENT

How To Get Over Your Fears 1

It Might Make You Live A More Carefree Life 7

Time Has The Potential To Heal Wounds Gradually. 21

Discovering Your Inner Strength To Overcome Limiting Beliefs 40

The Influence Of Positive Thoughts 53

How Well You're Meeting Your Basic Needs 74

The Significance Of Stereotyping, Growth Theories, And Errors. 89

Creating A Helpful Environment. 97

Self-Care And Reflection: Rejuvenate Yourself And Grow Rich 107

Putting Yourself Back Together 125

How To Get Over Your Fears

Consider your primary goal. Why are you still not done with it? The solution is simple if you're like most people: fear. The thing that is preventing you from taking action toward your goals is fear.

Fear need not keep us from being distracted or cause us to make excuses. Among the most liberating activities you can engage in is mastering the art of fearlessness.

It's simple to act as though fear doesn't affect you and to make up reasons for why you haven't reached your full potential. Embrace fear as a signal to act rather than as an excuse to stay still and run away from it. Consider your goal. You've given in if you let fear keep you from achieving your goals.

Fear of not knowing, fear of failing, and other common anxieties originate from the same place: the limiting beliefs that keep you stuck.

You can overcome fear and go toward the life you want with these ten actions.

The Psychology of Getting Rid of Fear

If you don't understand the basic concepts of fear and anxiety, learning how to overcome them may seem like a frightening idea. Prior to criticizing yourself for being nervous, remember that fear is a normal evolutionary response. You are receiving messages from your body and brain, even though it might not feel like it at the moment. It becomes easy to overcome fear once you know what the symptoms are.

Fear in the body

Phobias are another manifestation of physical anxiety; 12% of people have experienced a phobia at some point. An overwhelming fear of a particular situation, object, or animal is known as a phobia. Several well-known phobias include those of spiders, heights, public speaking, and cramped spaces.

Your respiration will quicken, and your pulse rate will elevate when you experience a body terror reaction. You can experience lightheadedness, sweating, a dry mouth, or a pit in your stomach. Your muscles can feel weaker or more rigid. All of these are results of the "fight or flight" response in your body. If you didn't experience the fear response, you would be far more open to danger. However, fear can manifest itself in a variety of ways in the modern world, some of which are less obvious.

Uncertainty

Consider anxiety as a chronic fear. Frequently, it is more concerned with the future than the here and now. In America, anxiety problems are becoming more prevalent: Every year, up to 18% of the population is affected. Stress and anxiety can have long-term effects: Your body releases a hormone known as cortisol when you are under stress.

An excess of cortisol can affect your immune system, impair your ability to sleep and focus, and even make you gain weight. Many of us experience generalized anxiety, which is characterized by difficulty falling asleep, difficulty focusing, and recurrently replaying the same scenarios in our minds.

Fear of not knowing

The Six Human Needs fundamentally drive our thoughts, deeds, and behaviours. For a great deal of us, our most pressing need is certainty: We're curious about what will happen next. We also require variance and unpredictability in our lives, even though we do need some regularity. We are prevented from stepping beyond our comfort zones by our dread of the unknown. "You might as well stay here, where it's safe," it advises us. It's the fundamental cause of the sense of being stuck and unable to achieve one's goals that many people experience.

Fear of not succeeding

An additional common worry that stems from people's need for significance and assurance is the fear of failing. We are hardwired to seek pleasure above suffering, and staying out of trouble is certainly a simple way to stay out of trouble. We all want to feel important, yet when we fail, we feel little and unimportant.

However, we are also predisposed to growth, and as any successful person in the world is aware, failure breeds innovation. One needs to modify their perspective on failure to see it as an advantage rather than a drawback.

How to get over your fears

Learning to control your fear response and turn it to your benefit is the first step toward conquering fear. Discovering your core is the first step towards combating fear. These are tried-and-true methods for overcoming anxiety and fear so you can live your life to the fullest.

Determine your concerns.

The process of conquering fear is similar to tackling any other kind of obstacle: in order to overcome it, you must first identify it. What is it that scares you? Take a few minutes to sit quietly and observe your feelings, ideas, and physical experiences. Put down as much detail as you can about what comes to mind. To gain more insight into your motivations, think about starting a regular mindfulness meditation practice. You'll feel more confident to face your fears as you uncover your inner self.

It Might Make You Live A More Carefree Life.

Living with low self-esteem is unpleasant enough, but when you're doing everything you can to get over those feelings, it can cause serious issues. If you're not careful, it can start small and grow like wildfire.

I engaged in several dangerous behaviours during my adolescent years when I struggled with poor self-esteem. I believed that I would feel beautiful if I was "model thin," therefore I missed meals. In addition, I experimented with drink and drugs because many with whom I socialized were involved in these activities. I believed that by taking part, I would win their approval.

Although I am aware that many teenagers face this issue, I can tell you from personal experience that risky activity won't make up for it. I went without food, but I was left feeling so weak and uncomfortable that I was hardly able to get through the day. When it was just me, myself, and I, I felt even more alone because I was trying to make other people like me more for what I did than for who I was.

It Will Impact Your Confidence in Yourself.

Let's return to the idea of the accomplished musician. They are competent and self-assured musicians, but let's imagine that they experienced a horrific event and failed to give themselves enough time to digest it. As they attempt to pick up the instrument, these doubts about themselves and all they do fill their minds. They are aware of their expertise, yet they are not as good as they previously were. They make obvious blunders or forget parts of the music, and this continues until they lose the confidence they had possessed.

Is Your Sense of Self-Worth Too High?

Yes, you might love yourself too much, but having a high sense of self-worth is rarely a bad thing. But what about the narcissists and individuals who are "full of themselves" who you may encounter? They must have such a strong sense of self-worth that it drives them to act as though everyone else is beneath them.

But what if that highly self-assured individual actually has very low or no self-esteem? When someone presents this significant image, it remains only that—an image. These people behave in this manner because they dislike certain aspects of themselves. Although you should respect yourself, keep in mind that the outside world also exists.

What Elements Strengthen or Weaken Your Self-Esteem?

Once more, there are a lot of reasons why you can think that you're the only person in the world going through difficult times. Although others understand, this is your journey.

Your past largely influences this feeling. Your upbringing has influenced everything that has moulded your identity and personality. This is going to be your starting point, and your surroundings will shape the remainder. Your perspective is the main obstacle in your path if your fundamental requirements are being provided and you are surrounded by love and support. However, the majority of your future self-esteem is shaped by your environment, which began the moment you were born.

Let us now examine the incidents that changed people's lives. You may be impacted by significant events such as natural catastrophes, war, social injustice, and others. This also holds for other traumatic experiences that are unique to you, such as poverty, abuse, or school bullying. If it qualifies as a traumatic incident, it will affect your sense of self-worth.

Conversely, significant accomplishments and the opposite of painful experiences will boost your self-esteem. The abilities you acquire to deal with traumatic situations or negative thoughts can also help you feel more confident. Being able to handle situations will help you navigate life's ups and downs.

Building Up Your Self-Esteem

I believe it's only right that I warn you upfront that it will not be simple to change your direction and cultivate a strong sense of self-worth. To maintain your momentum, you'll need a great deal of drive, perseverance, and self-control. The final element is crucial because, although you may feel like you can't go on at times, discipline will help you get through these difficult periods.

Essentially, this means that you must analyze your ideas, identify the ones that are critical of yourself, and begin to count them until you are able to replace them with constructive ones. Many of these self-defeating beliefs are instinctive, so until you can think more positively about yourself and the circumstances you find yourself in, you will need to think more deliberately.

There are a lot of things you may learn on your own or from the people you love and trust in order to love and accept who you are. However, these are just a handful of items that will set you on the correct path:

● Commence taking compliments. This will be difficult for me because, as someone who has battled poor self-esteem, I know how difficult it can be to receive praise or to adopt the "modesty" attitude. However, you need to be more receptive to other people's opinions if you ever want to persuade yourself that you are worthwhile.

● Be gentle with yourself. Once more, I understand. I know it's difficult not to punish yourself after you make a mistake, but you have to be kind to yourself. Nobody is flawless, and nobody ever does anything perfectly the first time. Therefore, give yourself some breathing room and keep in mind that life isn't flawless and that what matters is how we respond to it.

● Accept and love every aspect of who you are. Again, nobody is flawless, but that doesn't mean you have to stop loving the person you are. Everybody has defects, and it's critical to accept them. This demonstrates to the rest of the world that you take responsibility for your mistakes. Moreover, wouldn't you believe that a more moderate approach would be preferable if you were forced to live with these aspects of yourself that you find objectionable?

● See your worth in this world. Even while there are numerous opportunities to grow into new versions of ourselves throughout life, take a minute to accept and value the person you are right now. Once more, you will have many chances to develop into the person you truly want to be, but you shouldn't undervalue the amazing person you are right now.

Recognize the value of having a high sense of self-worth. You apply yourself and make an effort to obtain a decent grade on an exam because you recognize how important it is to do well. Self-esteem should be no different. You'll be more motivated to improve your self-esteem when you fully comprehend its significance for your development.

Start a thankfulness diary. Writing things down allows you to see things with your own eyes, even though, at first, it might seem absurd. It gives the ideas running through your head more authenticity. It doesn't have to be elaborate because the contents contain the key. Jot down anything good in your life. A pleasant moment from your day, your accomplishments, your character traits, the people around you—all of these would be excellent journal topics that will lift your self-esteem by allowing you to express yourself.

● Put your ideas down in writing. I would advise keeping a thankfulness diary apart from this if you choose to do both. Jot down anything that's on your mind and begin examining the factors that affect your sense of self-worth. This might be self-talk or things that you've been told by others that keep repeating in your thoughts. Positive or negative, make notes.

● Take care of yourself like you would your friends. Consider your closest buddy, and then picture yourself speaking negatively about them. Is that really what you would do to your closest friend? Obviously not, so why are you torturing yourself in that way? This is one more of those deliberate actions, but you'll get used to it eventually.

● Strive for advancement. To me, it always sounds so simple, but it's effective. Change if you're not happy with where you are at the moment. Your self-esteem will suffer greatly if you are not where you want to be personally. Use these additional suggestions to start looking for strategies to change your circumstances.

OTHER MODELS FOR SETTING GOALS

Although the three Rs (Realistic, Relevant, and Rewarding) and the three Cs (Clarity, Commitment, and Consistency) are well-known goal-setting models, you might also find the following other models useful:

Model of OKR Goal-Setting

Setting challenging goals and determining key outcomes that track advancement toward those goals are the main components of the Objectives and Key Outcomes approach, which was made popular by organizations like Google. It places a strong emphasis on organizational alignment and transparency.

WOOP Model of Goal-Setting

Gabrielle Oettingen created the four-step goal-setting process known as WOOP (Wish, Outcome, Obstacle, Plan). It entails deciding on a want or goal, visualizing the ideal result, thinking about potential roadblocks, and coming up with a detailed plan of action to get over them.

GROW Model of Goal-Setting

The acronym GROW, which stands for Goal, Reality, Options (or Obstacles), and Will (or Way Forward), is frequently used in coaching. It assists people in identifying their objectives, evaluating their situation, considering alternatives and potential fixes, and formulating a plan of action for the future.

Reverse Goal-Setting

With this method, you first visualize the outcome you want to achieve and then work backwards to identify the steps that must be taken to get there. You may make sure that your actions are in line with your final goal by beginning with the end in mind.

Threefold Power

Using this approach, three primary objectives or tasks are chosen to concentrate on at any given time. You can prevent overstretching yourself and improve your chances of achieving substantial progress in those areas by narrowing your attention to three goals.

Remember that the goal-setting model you use should make sense for you and your particular situation. To choose which strategy and model suits you the most, you can try out a variety of models. Seeking the advice of a life coach or therapist can also be a great way to get support and new perspectives on your goal-setting process if you're feeling overwhelmed or stuck.

Find the Purpose of Your Life in Chapter 3

What makes you happy? What makes you happy and passionate? Give this some thought for a moment. Maybe you have all these things you want to do, but because of everything else you have to get done every day, you never get around to doing any of them. It's alright, you're not by yourself! By identifying your life's purpose and discovering your passion, you can begin to live a more fulfilling existence. How to do it is as follows:

I. Write in a journal. Hopefully, you have already taken this step to record your previous successes and to keep track of the fears you have conquered. It's time to pick up that journal and write down your reasons for believing you are here on Earth, your passions, and the things that make you happy.

You should just write down your thoughts in this notebook, as it is exclusively for you. Don't try to be perfect. Your life path will become clear to you when you talk about the things you want to do with your life and are really honest with yourself.

II. Explore your hobbies more thoroughly. Talk about the moments in your life when you were truly joyful. Write about the individuals that pique your attention the most. Talk about your preferred way of spending time. Who are some of your role models? With just a week to live, how would you spend it? You can spend more time doing the things you are genuinely passionate about by using these suggestions to help you discover what those things are.

III. Talk about the people and places you cherish. This can help you discover more about the kind of life you wish to lead and clarify where your heart truly resides. If you had no restrictions, what would you be doing? Focusing on your passions reveals deeper passions than just the things you rationally value.

IV. Make a reverse plan. When you are 100 years old, how would you like your life to be? What would be your plan of action? What goals would you pursue? Put all of your goals down on paper if you want to lead a passionate life. Your life's passion lies somewhere along the journey.

You can write on the subjects mentioned above and then use that writing to create life goals. You'll achieve some of your aims tomorrow. Some may only be feasible in the distant future. You can have the life you want if you put in enough time, effort, and concentration.

Time Has The Potential To Heal Wounds Gradually.

When it comes to repairing the emotional scars left by unrequited love, time is an invaluable friend. This chapter, which is the fifth, will concentrate on how time can promote mental health and healing. The person can learn how wounds heal with time and attention, opening them to new experiences, opportunities for love, and personal development.

Grief's emotional journey

There are several stages involved in the extremely difficult process of mourning unrequited love. The person goes through these phases—from denial and rage to sadness and acceptance—under the guidance of time. Every phase offers a chance to work through feelings and make progress toward recovery.

The comfort that comes with time

The strong and overpowering feelings that come with unrequited love can eventually fade. The person may gradually feel less emotionally charged, which will enable them to view the situation more clearly and objectively. Time allows for the healing of wounds and the enlargement of perspective.

The reflective and educational process

Time gives people the chance to think about themselves and gain knowledge, in addition to allowing emotions to pass. With more healing under his belt, the person is able to look more critically at the experience of unfulfilled love. Finding limiting beliefs and behavioural patterns can open doors to emotional and personal development.

The significance of self-care in the process of recovery

In the period of recovery, self-care is crucial. Resilience can be strengthened by giving oneself occasional breaks and taking care of oneself both physically and emotionally. Learning to create appropriate boundaries and say "no" when necessary are other aspects of practising self-care. Taking care of oneself while going through the healing process is a sign of self-love.

The value of exercising self-compassion

There is no set timeline for the healing process, and it can differ from person to person. The person must learn to be patient with himself and let time pass without putting too much pressure on himself. It is a sign of care for oneself to acknowledge that emotional wounds take time to heal and that there is no time limit on when one should feel fully recovered.

companionship and emotional support during the journey

Having a network of emotional support is essential during the recovery process. To help you get through tough times, close friends, family, or even therapists can offer the company and support you need. Speaking with a trusted person about your feelings and experiences can be consoling and offer a fresh viewpoint on the circumstances.

The significance of self-reflection and acceptance

With time, the person can learn to accept what cannot be altered and engage in introspection. The person can learn to accept the circumstance as it is and discover opportunities to grow from it, as opposed to dwelling on the past or lamenting what might have been. To let go of unfavourable feelings and start the healing process, introspection and acceptance are essential first steps.

Make room for fresh possibilities.

Time also gives people the chance to create room in their lives for new opportunities. The heart is liberated from the burden of the past and opens itself to new emotional experiences as the wounds heal. You can demonstrate to yourself that being the object of unrequited love does not limit your capacity for love and love in return by being open to new relationships and connections.

Acquiring emotional fortitude

Over time, the healing process may also present a chance to strengthen emotional fortitude. Acquiring the ability to persevere in the face of difficulty and overcome obstacles might empower a person to take on new tasks with more assurance. Building emotional resilience is an important ability to have on the road to recovery.

In conclusion, wounds heal with time.

It is indisputable that time can mend the emotional scars left by unrequited love. Emotions become softer with time; the person develops emotionally, learns new things, and becomes more receptive to chances. Important components of this process include self-care, introspection, emotional support, and patience with yourself.

Time is an ally that helps a person get through the many stages of grief and toward a life that is more emotionally rich and rewarding. The person can eventually learn to accept the past, mend its scars, and look forward to the future with resiliency and optimism.

ADHD Subtypes and Characteristics

The following are the three main forms of ADHD:

1. The impulsive and hyperactive personality type: This personality type has a supercharged body and brain. The traits of this type of ADHD include impulsive behaviour, excessive activity, and trouble staying still. These are fearless individuals who are prepared to face any obstacle in the realm of ADHD.

Characteristics of Hyperactivity and Impulsivity

Taps or fidgets with hands, feet, or seat frequently.

Frequently, they get up from their seat as necessary, like at meetings or work.

Has a lot of restlessness.

Frequently unable to engage in peaceful activities.

They are "on the go" and behave as though they are "driven by a motor," which makes it difficult for them to sit still for extended periods, such as in meetings or dining establishments.

Often uses exaggerated language.

For instance, they frequently speak during talks before the issue is fully asked due to impatience.

May find it difficult to wait their turn, for example, in a line.

Frequently tampers with or agitates others by assuming their role or working alongside them, for example.

The phrase "Inattentive Type" is frequently employed to characterize individuals with Attention-Deficit/Hyperactivity Disorder (ADHD) whose primary symptoms are related to inattention.

One indication of ADHD could be inattention.

People frequently make careless mistakes at work, such as omitting important information or failing to pay close attention to details, which leads to inaccurate output.

Frequently finds it difficult to focus when doing things like reading for lengthy periods or going to lectures or seminars.

For example, when addressed immediately and without any obvious disturbances, he doesn't seem to be listening.

For example, frequently starts a task at work just to become sidetracked or lose focus, which results in following instructions incorrectly and leaving unfinished projects behind.

Often has trouble keeping tasks and/or activities organized; examples include not using effective time management, keeping supplies and items organized, arranging work in a sequential fashion, or missing deadlines.

Usually stays away from or despises mentally taxing tasks like writing reports or completing out paperwork.

Frequently lose items that are necessary for their professions or hobbies, like a phone, wallet, handbag, or spectacles. Easily distracted by trivial stimuli. Adults might encounter this in addition to unrelated concepts.

Never remembers to do small things like pick up the phone.

3. A single category is created by combining the signs of inattention and hyperactivity-impulsivity. There are numerous ways that symptoms of compounded ADHD could appear. Imagine a person who varies between being outgoing and inattentive, much like many songs on the radio. Before they start to bounce off the walls, they may need a minute to regain focus. Since they are juggling twelve occupations at once, they could find it difficult to get into a routine.

Characteristics of the ADHD Combination Type

A combination of symptoms from the inattentive and hyperactive-impulsive categories characterize it. The following are some of the most crucial traits of the ADHD combo type:

Inattention: People who have ADHD-C frequently struggle to concentrate, pay attention to small details, and avoid careless mistakes. They could have trouble managing their time and responsibilities, and they might frequently forget or misplace things that are required to complete daily chores.

This subtype also exhibits impulsivity and hyperactivity. They may frequently fidget, tap their hands or feet, or struggle to sit still, especially when it's required.

Impulsivity: People with ADHD-C frequently display impulsivity. People could find it difficult to wait their turn, answer clumsily, participate fully in conversations, or wait their turn.

Problems with self-control: People with combination type ADHD may have trouble controlling their emotions and impulses. They could have trouble managing their emotions and exhibit mood swings in a variety of situations.

These individuals frequently struggle with executive function deficiencies, which include issues with time management, organizing, planning, and initiating tasks. This could affect your personal, professional, and academic lives.

Social issues: A person with ADHD-C could find it difficult to communicate with other people. Impulsivity and a lack of self-control can lead to social issues such as talking over other people or not waiting your turn in group activities.

People with combo-type ADHD frequently experience difficulties in the workplace and the classroom because of their impulsivity, hyperactivity, and impulsiveness. They might struggle to complete tasks, follow instructions, and meet deadlines.

Emotional dysregulation: Mood swings and emotional sensitivity are common among individuals with ADHD who are Combination type. They can find it difficult to restrain their anger and bitterness.

Given that ADHD-C frequently co-occurs with other conditions like anxiety, depression, and learning challenges, diagnosing and treating it may be more difficult.

TAKE UP A PASSION OR OTHER PASSIONS YOU LIKE TO DO

You can never have high self-esteem if you spend your entire day doing something you loathe every morning when you wake up. Either look for a better job or make an effort to value what you are doing. In some instances, changing careers will be advantageous despite the fact that it can be a little uncomfortable. Participating in fun activities can help you feel better about yourself in a number of ways. You can feel more confident and satisfied when you are doing something you are good at, which can help you recognize your skills and abilities.

Furthermore, engaging in enjoyable activities leads to interactions with people who value your skills or share your interests, which can validate your abilities and give you a sense of significance. Positive feedback and acknowledgement are two additional benefits of engaging in enjoyable activities. Participating in activities you enjoy also gives you the freedom to express yourself, allowing your uniqueness and creativity to flow. This can help you feel authentic and more confident in your skills. Furthermore, engaging in enjoyable hobbies can lead to personal development since you'll be able to see your progress when you put time and effort into something you love.

Last but not least, doing things you enjoy makes you happier and more fulfilled. It also helps you see yourself and your skills favourably, which raises your self-esteem. In summary, engaging in activities you enjoy can lead to a feeling of success, compliments, self-expression, personal development, and joyful experiences—all of which can contribute to higher self-esteem.

Accept your body, mind, and spirit.

Respecting your body, mind, and spirit is the only way you can truly accept who you are. It's crucial to lead a healthy lifestyle if you value your body. Give off cigarettes, alcohol, and everything else that is unhealthy for you. It doesn't matter what it is. Go to the gym for at least three hours every week. When your muscles start to grow, you'll not only feel incredible but also like your muscles are being used to their maximum capacity, which will increase your self-esteem and confidence. Read literature if you want to nourish your mind and soul.

Putting your strengths front and centre: You can cultivate a good self-image and value your distinctive attributes by highlighting your abilities and accomplishments.

Recognizing outside validation Getting affirmation from others in the form of compliments, praise, and acknowledgement can serve as a reminder of your value and merit.

This is known as self-compassion.

Making self-care a priority: Looking after all facets of your health shows respect for yourself and improves your sense of value in general.

Establishing and completing meaningful goals: Achieving meaningful goals boosts your self-esteem by proving your skills and abilities.

Setting up sensible limits: Declaring your limits wants, and desires makes it clear how valuable you are and demands the respect you are due. Your aggressiveness reinforces your self-worth.

In summary, one effective strategy for raising your self-esteem is to embrace your body, mind, and soul. It entails developing goals, flourishing and, making and accomplishing objectives, prioritizing self-care, practising self-compassion, and realizing your worth.

Maintaining our mental and emotional health, in addition to our outward look, is essential to developing self-esteem. In order to establish self-esteem, we must embrace our mind and soul.

Develop self-awareness. Consider your feelings, ideas, and actions. Recognize your areas of strength and improvement. You may change for the better and gain confidence with this self-awareness.

Prioritize your development and make time for introspection, learning, and personal growth. Investing in your development and learning new abilities might help you feel more confident.

SELF-POSITIVE TALK

Give yourself a self-pat on the back. When you succeed, take pride in your accomplishment rather than attributing it to chance. Never assume that your success was the result of pure luck. Yes, there might be some other influences, but you were the one who worked so hard. Write down your successes if you still don't think it's real, but don't go crazy and start acting conceited.

Recognize your negative ideas; start by recognizing the self-talk or negative thoughts that you find yourself thinking about on a regular basis. Keep an eye out for the particular words or statements that depress you, like "I'll never succeed," "I'm not good enough," or "I make mistakes a lot."

Contest the legitimacy: Once you've identified these negative ideas, critically evaluate their integrity. Consider whether you have any hard data to back up these beliefs. You will frequently discover that they are predicated on presumptions, fears, or experiences from the past that might not fully reflect your current situation.

Look for other viewpoints. Now, actively look for opposing viewpoints or arguments to refute your pessimistic beliefs. If you feel, for instance, that "I'm not good enough," consider your prior accomplishments or victories which defy this idea. Seek out proof that highlights your advantages, skills, or good traits.

Substitute with uplifting statements. After you've determined other viewpoints, swap out the negative ideas with encouraging ones. Make a list of affirmations that you can use to counteract your negative self-talk. To strengthen positive self-beliefs, repeat these affirmations on a regular basis.

Discovering Your Inner Strength To Overcome Limiting Beliefs

When you have narrow-minded beliefs and fail to comprehend the big picture, those around you will perceive you as narrow-minded. This is something that women are quick to notice, and being overly conservative or narrow-minded is not appealing at all. Marrying a man who is always correct or whose strong beliefs overpower others is not what women desire in a spouse. They are looking for someone eager to listen, learn, and be open to changing his mind.

You own amazing power within yourself. It's possible that you haven't yet realized how swiftly you can break bad behaviours. Write down your entrenched ideas and be honest with yourself if you have been accused of being narrow-minded. The following are examples of the common beliefs that you might find on this list: ● I am a Democrat ● I don't believe in God ● I don't believe in life after death ● I don't believe in the tooth fairy.

Well, the last one may have been a little extreme, but you get the idea. If you think that things are predetermined, you won't be open to comprehending other individuals, and ladies detest opinionated guys who stick to their narrow viewpoints. Marianna thought she had met the one, but she quickly bid him farewell when he insisted that a woman should not go out and pursue a career because that wasn't what she believed. You have to realize that viewpoints are somewhat similar to butts. Everybody has one, but forcing yours on others makes you extremely limiting the number of people who would genuinely be interested in conversing with you, let alone dating you.

For the next few weeks, I want you to engage in conversations, turn off your strong opinions, and learn how to listen to other people. Even while some of what you hear might be absurd, remember that it's their absurdity, so try not to take it personally unless it directly impacts you. Rather than doing that, attempt to ascertain the meaning underlying the claims that people make. What is sympathetic in this situation? Why would he say that? Why does she look bitter? What is wrong with adjusting my perspective?

Sympathy and empathy are unrelated concepts. It entails having the capacity to put oneself in another person's shoes and consider situations from their viewpoint. As a result, if you begin to do this and have narrow ideas, a whole new universe where you have a deeper understanding of people will open up. I'll give you an illustration. Nancy was hoping to go to the movies with Charles. She became quite furious and hated the movies. He sat her down and listened to her story, not demanding to go, even though he had no idea why. As it turned out, she had never been approached by a man who tried to push himself on her in the theatre. He could see why she didn't want to leave, but he offered her every reason to trust him by progressively removing any doubt from her mind. She eventually stopped finding going to the movies to be such a hassle. You have to realize that her decision to go to a different place would have angered Charles, and his closed-mindedness might have caused the relationship to terminate. Keep your mouth open. Be open-minded and avoid drawing incorrect judgments from events.

Even if this is all in your head, you should always ask yourself why. People act in certain ways for a variety of reasons. Your ability to be adaptable and make a woman feel as though her tale matters more than yours gives you a power that you have never had before. That's a fantastic way to begin a relationship. Because you bothered to listen rather than voice your opinion, you could eventually even be able to work things out with a woman. Permitting her to keep hers will let you get to know her better, and information is power!

7 THINGS YOU NEED TO KNOW ABOUT FEAR

Fear may be debilitating and uncomfortable. However, eliminating it would be the equivalent of putting down your home alarm system because it occasionally produces loud and uncomfortable noises.

Being loyal does not imply being ruthless. To be fearless, one must understand how to age gracefully. You need to know a few things about what you're dealing with in order to accomplish that.

1. Slender and well-nourished.

Experiencing fear is neither unusual nor a sign of weakness: The ability to be tolerant is a component of typical brain function. Actually, a lack of fear could indicate severe brain damage.

2. Many Hades Bring Fur.

FEAR is an essentially unpalatable experience that can range from mild to traumatic—from waiting for the outcome of a medical examination to learning of a terrible terrorist strike. Horrifying experiences can permanently mark your brain, necessitating professional assistance. Chronic stress, on the other hand, is a low-intensity form of anxiety that can manifest itself as restless anxiety, ongoing worry, and everyday uneasiness. It can subtly but definitely impair your physical and mental well-being over time.

3. Fear Is Not As Uniform as You May Think.

Fur is a combination of taught, learned, and intuitive. Certain fields are inflammatory: For instance, the parachute causes anxiety mostly due to its practical implications for survival. Further fears are discovered: We acquired the skill of becoming fearful of specific individuals, locations, or circumstances due to unfavourable associations and past experiences. For example, every time you come too close to a body of water, a near-drowning incident may cause fear. Other fears are raised: Cultural norms frequently dictate whether or not something is appropriate to fear. Consider, for instance, how some social groupings are feared and punished due to a perception cultivated by society that they pose a threat.

4. You Can Be Saved Without Being in Peril.

Fear is also imagined, which is why it might appear as something frightening. Actually, because of the efficiency of our brains, we start to fear a variety of stimuli that are either not frightening (conditioned fear) or not even there (anticipatory anxiety). We were alarmed by what we imagined would occur. According to some neuroscientists, humans are the most fearsome creatures on the planet because of our capacity for thought, learning, and fear-making. However, this mild, innocuous fear has the potential to develop into a chronic, unspecific anxiety that can become debilitating.

5. The more afraid you are, the more terrified you will feel.

If you are already experiencing fear, your fear response is amplified through a procedure known as phobia. Even seemingly insignificant events look frightening when you're ready for fear. When watching a documentary about venomous spiders, you might be startled and jump out of your seat in the front of the room by a tickle on your neck (caused, perhaps, by a loose thread in your sweater). Even light aircraft turbulence will force your blood pressure through the plane's roof if you are afraid of flying. The more anxious you are about the security of your job, the more you will worry when your boss calls you in for even an inconvenient meeting.

6. The Actions You Perform Are Farmed.

Fear-motivated behaviours fall into one of four categories: fear, fear, fear, or fear. Freeze refers to stopping what you're doing and concentrating on the relevant stimuli to decide what to do next (for example, reading a document stating that your company would be laying off employees). Next, you select between light or dark. You choose to either confront the issue head-on (convince your bosses why you shouldn't be fired) or work around it (search for another job). When the fear overwhelms you, you experience flight: You don't flee or fight; in reality, you do nothing. Instead, you mope, meditate, and become fixated on the problem without taking any action. Chronic fatigue syndrome can result in both hopelessness and despair.

7. The MoreRealThe Threat, The MoreHeroicYourActions.

When faced with real or imagined threats, our responses vary. Impaired threats lead to paralysis. Worrying about all the bad things that might or might not happen in the future causes you to worry a lot but not take any action. You're stuck in a state of fear, feeling overwhelmed and unsure of what to do. Conversely, real threats result in a frenzy. When the threat is obvious and urgent, you react quickly and without hesitation. This explains why people are far more likely to alter their eating habits following a serious health event (such as a heart attack) than following facts on the harmful effects of a diet high in fat foods. You must put yourself in danger if you wish to mobilize your troops.

Being Kind to Yourself This is the most significant section of the book. You cannot sustain kindness on the outside if you are unable to cultivate kindness within. Our relationship with ourselves is the foundation of all partnerships. You cannot identify insensitivity or outright cruelty toward others if you are unable to identify when you are being unkind to yourself. A lot of us don't even realize we talk to ourselves in this way.

The first and most crucial step in practising kindness is becoming conscious of the words we use to speak to ourselves. Try printing a picture of yourself when you were around four years old if you are having problems being compassionate toward yourself. This will remind you of your inner kid and help you recall who you are and who lives inside of you. Some people might need to repent by listening to the words of their abusive father. Even though we might be engaged in internal conflict, recognizing them is the first step in bringing about long-lasting, constructive transformation.

Stress frequently manifests as a physical symptom that alerts us to the moment when our negative ideas start to take root. After taking three deep breaths and repeating your affirmation with loving care, you will gently acknowledge your inner critic. This will stop the neural network, a circuit in your brain that fires continuously. We are rewiring the circuits by using affirmation, deep breathing, and loving-kindness to interrupt these loops. Our experiences in life have conditioned us to link external stimuli to emotional emotions. By becoming aware of them and treating ourselves with compassion, we can break through these "thought-to-feeling" circuits.

Our thoughts can be rewired to adopt more positive viewpoints by repeating affirmations that serve as a reminder of our actual values and capabilities. By applying neuroplasticity to our benefit, sincerity, discipline, and repetition can shape our thoughts. Your inward compassion will shape your interactions with all other life.

The Influence Of Positive Thoughts

In this chapter, we'll look at how self-beliefs are fundamental to developing strong self-esteem. We'll learn how to develop more uplifting thoughts to improve your perception of yourself.

Beliefs' Significance for Self-Esteem

Your self-beliefs greatly influence your self-perception and, by extension, your self-esteem. Your sense of worthiness for love, prosperity, and happiness increases the likelihood that your self-esteem is in good shape.

Contrasting Positive and Negative Beliefs:

- Negative Beliefs: These are ideas that make you feel less than good about yourself. "I'm a failure" and "I'm not good enough" are two examples.

- Positive Beliefs: These are convictions that uphold your sense of worth and identity. "I am capable" and "I deserve success" are two examples.

How to Develop Hopeful Thoughts:

1. Self-awareness: Recognize the false assumptions you hold. The first step in changing them is realizing they exist.

2. Questioning: Consider if your beliefs are the result of erroneous reasoning or factual information. Negative ideas frequently exaggerate and don't correspond with reality.

3. Replacement: Change your negative thoughts to constructive ones. Refute any negative belief that comes up with a positive one.

4. Visualization and Affirmations: To help you believe what you want to believe, use affirmations and visualization. Repeat encouraging statements to yourself every day and picture yourself succeeding.

5. Celebrate Your Success: Give yourself credit for any accomplishment, no matter how tiny.

This supports the development of optimistic beliefs.

Exercise for Practice: Positive Thoughts Journal

Keep a journal in which you note any unpleasant thoughts that come up during the day. Next, refute those assumptions and substitute more optimistic ones. Monitor your development over time.

Knowing About Self-Sabotage

Negative beliefs can frequently cause self-sabotage. For instance, you might pass up difficult chances if you think you're incapable. To overcome this self-sabotage, one must acknowledge it.

The Effects of Positive Thoughts:

Your relationship with the world and your sense of self-worth will shift as you develop more positive self-beliefs. You'll have greater self-assurance, resilience, and receptivity to new chances.

Recall that it takes time to transform negative thoughts into positive ones, but the effort is well worth it. Unwavering self-esteem is based on your own belief in yourself.

We will discuss how to handle criticism and judgment in the upcoming chapter, as these are critical abilities for preserving a healthy sense of self-worth.

APPROACHING REALITY

Recognizing Authenticity and Its Advantages

Before setting out on an authentic journey, we need to address these important questions first: What does the self consist of? Authenticity: what is it?

In his essay, The Influence of Self-Awareness on Human Behavior (1979), psychology professor Robert Wicklund of the University of Texas at Austin addressed the effects of self-awareness on behaviour. He covered a number of conflicting facets of self-awareness.

According to this definition of the self, before a self-component can be said to have a substantial influence on psychological functioning, it must first become the focus of the individual. Until attention is directed inward, the self-components are mostly inactive and do not affect an individual's psychological condition (p. 187).

According to Wicklund, the self is made up of a combination of recognized, reportable active activities as well as automatic behaviours that are driven by latent subconscious traits. We are limited to describing the outward manifestations of our unique selves when we try to explain our characteristics. This suggests that until we intentionally and exploratorily think about the aspects of ourselves that are hidden from conscious consciousness, we will never truly comprehend the breadth of our unique personalities.

A person who dedicates a larger portion of their time to introspection is said to be self-aware. Additionally, they possess the capacity to perceive themselves through the eyes of others, thus employing them as a kind of mirror. Understanding how we fit into the world in relation to societal standards and expectations makes this a crucial ability.

Within the context of self-awareness, authenticity refers to the state of being true to our views, values, and personalities without masks or pretences. It entails accepting one's flaws as well as strengths and coordinating words and deeds with one's innermost sentiments and ideas. An authentic connection with oneself and others is fostered by this alignment, which makes for a more contented and grounded life experience.

Research in the psychological domain has demonstrated a strong correlation between authenticity and self-worth. More of the other is encouraged by each. In order to better understand the implications of each factor in personal satisfaction with oneself and to address the question, "What influences the way that people feel about themselves from day to day?" one such study looked at the interconnectivity between daily self-esteem, need satisfaction, and authenticity. Heppner & associates, 2008).

Over two weeks, 116 people participated in Heppner's study. Every day, each of the three variables was applied to a participant, and their stated self-perception was tracked for any changes. This means that even after taking into account a range of contrasting emotions (including negative ones), the complex connections between feeling a sense of truth in oneself, feeling independent, believing oneself to have a high level of skill, and feeling meaningfully connected to others positively affect how people feel about themselves in daily life. This study tested for and proved the existence of these connections.

Furthermore, the Heppner et al. study (2008) found that: "Our findings indicate that people who feel competent and socially connected feel better about themselves overall." That isn't the full picture, though. Doing everyday actions in a way that reflects one's integrity and choice is also crucial for a daily sense of self-worth (p. 1144).

Since choice is a reflection of our self-perceived identity and abilities, it is an essential component of self-confidence. Making decisions that are consistent with our true selves comes easy to us when we act on our true needs and desires. Therefore, practising authenticity strengthens relationships and confidence, and the presence of meaningful interpersonal connections and self-esteem reinforces authenticity itself.

Three Procedures for Leaving Your Comfort Zone Step 1: Determine Your Comfort Zone Start by evaluating the limits of your comfort zone introspectively.

Which facets of your job, personal life, or choices have grown accustomed and routine? Determine the places where your sense of security may be keeping you from facing problems. This awareness creates the foundation for focused development.

Step 2: Create Gradual Difficulties

Instead of diving headfirst into suffering, take a step toward gradual growth. Establish manageable yet challenging goals that gradually take you beyond of your comfort zone. Whether it's networking gatherings, public speaking, or picking up a new skill, these managed discomforts increase your threshold for the strange.

Step 3: Accept Education and Adjustment

Accept the idea that moving outside of your comfort zone will lead to learning and development rather than instant mastery. Accept mistakes as learning experiences and obstacles as chances to improve your strategy.

You'll have allies in adaptability and resilience as you make your way through unfamiliar discomfort zones.

You can increase your comfort zone and improve your capacity for "Think Rich, Grow Rich" by implementing these strategies. Remember that the depth of experience and transformation you acquire when you travel into unfamiliar territory is a treasure that cannot be compared to the safety of the familiar.

Chapter 2.3: Embracing a Supportive Environment Introduction: Embracing a Supportive Environment Within "Think Rich, Grow Rich: Building a Mindset for Wealth Creation," the chapter "Surrounding Yourself with Support" stands out as a vital theme. Here, we discover the significant impact of the community and the relationships we cultivate.

1. Fostering Assistive Connections

Building a network of support starts with developing connections based on trust, respect, and common ground. Look for people who share your goals, push your ideas, and acknowledge your accomplishments. This can be friends who provide emotional support, peers who offer companionship, or mentors who offer direction. In my personal life, I've learned the importance of interacting with people from all backgrounds because they all bring a different viewpoint to my path. Creating an atmosphere that allows for the flourishing of varied ideas can lead to innovative thinking and significant progress.

2. Taking Part in Valuable Conversations

It takes more than just association to surround oneself with support; it takes genuine interchange. Participate actively in discussions that pique your interest, extend your perspective, and present you with fresh prospects. This could be taking part in networking activities, mastermind groups, or lectures. I've discovered that by putting myself in situations where individuals are willing to offer their knowledge and experiences, I've learned priceless lessons that have shaped the way I create money. Keep in mind that a healthy network is a two-way street; give as freely as you receive in terms of knowledge and support.

Section Two

3. Promoting a Culture of Development

The people you surround yourself with should foster a growth-oriented and cooperative culture. Create an atmosphere where people support one another, acknowledge successes, and remain resilient in the face of adversity. This growth-oriented culture can permeate not just your social circle but also your town, place of employment, and online spaces.

Throughout my path, I have seen firsthand how teamwork can result in exponential advancement. Adopting a growth-oriented mindset cultivates an ecosystem in which generating money is not solely a personal endeavour but rather a shared path towards prosperity.

Conclusion: Using Supportive Networks to Increase Wealth Creation The skill of surrounding oneself with support is more than just making contacts; it involves establishing an environment that is conducive to the development of your financial success and mindset. You add new insights, constant support, and priceless wisdom to your journey by cultivating connections that test, encourage, and inspire. In the chapter "Surrounding

Yourself with Support" of "Think Rich, Grow Rich: Building a Mindset for Wealth Creation," it is emphasized that creating money is not an isolated undertaking but rather a harmonious combination of mutual understanding, teamwork, and the enduring power of a supporting community. As you include these strands into your path, keep in mind that your network is a living, breathing catalyst that enhances your ability to think richly and, eventually, to become richer than just a list of names.

Achieve your goals little by little, and acknowledge each accomplishment.

While achieving large goals may appear challenging, it becomes much easier when broken down into manageable activities or phases. Smaller tasks or goals are easier to accomplish, and acknowledging and appreciating each accomplishment increases one's self-worth and confidence.

Develop a productive response to criticism.

You will undoubtedly encounter criticism at various points and phases of your life. Refrain from taking criticism personally, and instead, use it to identify your areas of weakness and progress. It will raise your self-esteem in addition to strengthening your resilience and assisting you in overcoming obstacles.

Gain problem-solving abilities to get over challenges.

Challenges and barriers are inevitable aspects of existence. Instead of giving up because of these difficulties, learn how to solve problems and get past them. Knowing that you can make decisions and handle challenging situations makes you feel more confident and improves your self-esteem.

Make sure your surroundings are filled with encouraging statements.

Keep some inspirational quotations and positive affirmations on posters or bulletin boards in your space. Additionally, write out some positive affirmations and read them out loud. These sayings and affirmations highlight that nothing is impossible and that all of your dreams are attainable.

Look for mentors or role models who motivate you. Mentors are a priceless resource that helps us understand many facets of life, navigate difficult and difficult circumstances, control our emotions, and build our personalities. Having a mentor increases your self-esteem by giving you more confidence in your abilities.

Accept your individuality.

You have to realize that you are an individual with your personality, set of skills, and attributes. Your confidence and self-esteem are substantially increased when you have the feeling that "I Am Unique," which gives you the ability to think favourably about yourself, recognize your value, and accept who you are.

Acknowledge your errors and move on.

Errors are inevitable and cannot be prevented. Errors occur in every human endeavour. Analyze our errors and draw lessons from them rather than constantly feeling sorry for them.

Acknowledging mistakes

Everyone has setbacks in life, but the truly courageous individuals are those who get back up and keep going for their goals. Always view setbacks as teaching moments, using them to reflect on what went wrong and what you should do differently the next time. The inventor of the lightbulb, Thomas Edison, is among the most renowned instances of learning from errors.

Cultivate thankfulness by listing your blessings. Recognize the good things in life and be grateful for what you have every day. And give thanks to the cosmos for whatever you own. Having gratitude helps you turn your attention from the things you lack to the things you do have and from the bad things in your life to the good things. Writing down your appreciation every day will improve your general well-being, lower stress levels, and help you adopt a more optimistic view of life.

Steer clear of harmful relationships that depress you.

You should immediately start avoiding anyone in your life who is putting you down, acting in a negative way toward you, and offering you no support. You should avoid these folks at all costs for your mental and physical health. These individuals may badly impact your self-esteem.

Consider your advantages rather than your disadvantages.

Every person has both innate strengths and shortcomings. Turn your attention from your flaws to your strengths, and examine your deficiencies to identify opportunities for development and potential solutions. Maintaining a constant focus on your shortcomings might cause your self-esteem to decline while highlighting your virtues can increase it.

Maintain proper posture; it will increase your self-assurance.

Since body language conveys our thoughts and emotional state, it is a crucial component of existence. Positivity in your posture improves your self-esteem and alters how other people perceive you.

Make a list of your achievements and refer to it frequently.

You could lose sight of your achievements when you are preoccupied with day-to-day tasks, difficulties, and disappointments. Make a list of all your accomplishments, even the little ones, and review and remind yourself of them often. When you doubt your talents, this can give you a much-needed confidence boost. Additionally, you'll be able to grow a sense of accomplishment and deservingness that will boost your confidence and inspire you.

Give your ideals and convictions some thought.

One of the most crucial and effective tools for developing oneself and raising one's level of awareness is self-reflection. Take some time to reflect on your views and values, and consider whether your objectives are consistent with them. Making more pertinent and meaningful decisions and choices that lead to a more authentic and fulfilling existence is made easier with the aid of self-reflection.

Change takes time, so have patience.

When it comes to reaching your objectives, changing your life, and growing yourself, always have compassion and patience for yourself because these things take time. To attain your goals, set reasonable expectations, deadlines, and goals.

Recognize that no one is flawless, including yourself. Since nobody is flawless, you must know that you are also imperfect. Seeking perfection results in a great deal of tension and mental uncertainty. Recognize that you might never be able to achieve perfection. Recognize and embrace your flaws, and remember that these are what set you apart from the rest of the world.

How Well You're Meeting Your Basic Needs….

Maslow's hierarchy of needs states that before we can satiate higher-level needs like self-actualization, esteem, and belongingness, we must first satiate our basic physiological and safety needs. This implies that you can find it challenging to meet your esteem demands if your physiological and safety needs are not satisfied.

For instance, someone may be more concerned about surviving if they are having difficulty meeting their fundamental needs for food, shelter, and safety. They may lack the mental and emotional capacity to take part in self-esteem-boosting activities like setting and achieving objectives for themselves or focusing on their positive traits. They could even receive harsh criticism from their inner critic for not meeting these requirements "better."

In addition, if a person's social requirements are not satisfied, they could find it difficult to grow a positive sense of self. A person's self-esteem may suffer if they believe they are alone or excluded from social groups, as this may make them feel less valuable and incapable of accomplishing their objectives.

A person's capacity to meet their esteem needs and cultivate a positive sense of self-worth may be hindered if their basic physiological and safety needs, as well as their social needs, are not satisfied. Because of this, your basic needs must be satisfied in order to provide a strong basis for your future personal development.

Our Prospects for the Future

Individuals who suffer from low self-esteem typically see things negatively in the future. This may have an impact on one aspect of their lives at a time or on their entire future.

For instance, a person may have great expectations for their professional prospects and growth. They might, however, decide that they are too ugly to pursue their desire of finding a devoted spouse.

People who have a healthy sense of self-worth typically look forward to the future with optimism. They believe that there will eventually be light at the end of the tunnel despite the fact that the journey is filled with obstacles and crises. Even while everything might not go as planned, they will still come out stronger and happier as a result. As a result, when faced with uncertainty or setbacks, they frequently exhibit a more proactive and problem-solving mindset.

Our Capacity to Establish Limits

Boundaries are a crucial component of self-esteem because they influence how other people view you. It also influences the lengths we will go to win over people.

Lack of boundary-setting skills leads people to prioritize the needs, objectives, and beliefs of others over their own. We're not suggesting depriving them of sleep for a single night to help them move past a breakup or a nasty sickness. We are discussing topics such as:

● Working triple shifts and showing up late for an unappreciative supervisor.
● Giving up your much-needed vacation deposit in order to watch someone else while they attend a concert.
● Giving up on their ambition to be writers or artists because their parents tell them that's "not a real job."
● Using the last $20 they had left over for gas to buy snacks for someone who isn't hungry but could use some right now.
Permit a roommate to disparage their religion—or lack thereof—on a regular basis.

- Make themselves go on dates with someone they don't want to in order to live up to cultural or parental expectations.
- Changing clothes and cutting off a favourite haircut because a partner or parent believes it makes them look more beautiful.

Individuals who possess a good sense of self-worth are typically able to decline requests that begin to belittle them as unique individuals. They still want and value the other person's favour, but not at the price of their own needs, dignity, or personal convictions. Even though saying "no" could disappoint some, they are usually more at ease expressing their requirements.

How Self-Esteem Is Measured

Numerous worksheets, surveys, and examinations are available to gauge one's level of self-esteem. Some have an age range of 9 to 12, such as the Piers-Harris Children's Self-Concept Scale. Some, such as Saraswat's Self-

Concept Questionnaire (SCQ) and the Behavioral Academic Self-Esteem Scale, are for certain domains or sectors. Some, like the Self-Esteem Stability Scale (SESS), measure how stable and fluctuating your self-esteem is.

Tests from periodicals, social media games, and other sources should not be taken unless they state that they are based on a validated test or were created by a recognized psychologist with expertise in this area. These exams are typically more recreational or have been penned by someone with a cursory knowledge of psychological theory. A good test will frequently come with an explanation of how it was tested and an official study report of its performance across several test groups.

Because the Rosenberg Self-Esteem Scale is valid across age, gender, region, and culture, it is regarded as the gold standard for measuring overall self-esteem. Ten statements about oneself are given, and you are asked to score how much you agree with each one. A copy of the test is located in the back of this book!

Keeping a Journal Can Help You Identify Thought Patterns

To acquire a rough sense of your self-esteem, you do not require these more formal measurements. You can also journal how your inner critic speaks to you during the day for a week or two. When the housework gets neglected, do they become the ugliest? Do they make you feel anxious when you are going to attempt anything new? Do they show you kindness and support as you handle a crisis at work? Do you have a sense of excitement and assurance just before starting something new? Have you ever been so afraid that your friend may leave you for no reason at all if you refuse to do them a favour? You can see trends in your self-worth, confidence, and the highs and lows of your self-esteem by keeping a journal of all these experiences.

To assist you in identifying the questions to ask and the mental processes to trace the origins of these beliefs and reconstruct the ones that undermine your self-worth, it would be ideal if you shared this journal with a therapist or certified counsellor. It can also be quite beneficial to share it with a reliable buddy!

Assessing your self-esteem is a crucial step in determining how confident and worthy you feel about yourself. Self-esteem may be measured and tracked on a regular basis, which will help you feel better about yourself and lead a more satisfying life.

There are more things you can do! We'll go over numerous strategies for boosting and mending your self-esteem in the upcoming chapter.

The Delusion of Personal Worth

As was previously discussed, there are a number of factors that influence self-esteem. The following can be used to simplify and break down these aspects:

- External Look • Sense of Perception
- Contentment in your Emotions • Your Objectives and Your Mission
- Environment and Outside Factors

We will discuss each of these points in great depth. We shall investigate both the external and internal elements that impact these five aspects.

Outward Look

This has to do with your self-perception of how you feel about your body and its physical attributes. This covers features like your weight, the colour of your eyes and hair, the contours of your face, your nose, and your entire body.

We should take into account the fact that physical beauty is quite important in this day and age. People work out for hours at the gym, and each year, millions of dollars are spent on anti-ageing and skin care products, not to mention cosmetic surgery, which is done to improve one's appearance.

Nowadays, it's also becoming more and more typical for individuals to visit health spas and beauty salons for soothing massages, manicures, and pedicures in addition to facials. Many guys can also be found visiting health spas among these patrons.

In addition to the internal elements, such as how you see yourself, there are a lot of external influences that have an impact on appearance and contribute significantly to our sense of self-worth. The media continuously bombards us with many representations of what individuals should look like.

A greater awareness of fashion has also emerged in people, some of whom are quite young. However, fashion is ever-evolving, so what was "in" yesterday could not be the next big thing. Therefore, staying up to date with the current trends might occasionally be difficult. For some, this may mean increased pressure.

From an early age, we are also typically conditioned to feel that certain things about our looks, dress code, social position, and behaviour are acceptable in society.

As a result, we learn early on that everyone should "look a certain way," as well as dress and behave in a particular way. When puberty strikes, we are so prone to self-consciousness that a lot of youngsters join fitness centres, go on diets, or adopt particular lifestyles.

When we start working and find ourselves going to beauty salons and health spas, as well as purchasing different skincare and anti-ageing products, all in an attempt to maintain a certain "level" of physical appearance and to look younger, that is when the next phase begins, and by then we have probably made it through puberty.

Our physical appearance is highly valued, and many people don't seem to understand the effects this has on one's self-esteem. This emphasis is especially to blame for the low self-esteem that many people experience. The impact on a person's self-esteem may be severe.

Although it is undeniable that physical beauty has a legitimate position in our lives, we should never allow it to serve as the primary criterion by which we judge our level of attractiveness, personal deservingness, pleasure, or success.

In summary, your level of self-esteem can be determined by your perception of your appearance and your feelings towards your body. One's self-esteem may eventually be made or broken by this.

Own it, live it, and be proud of who you are!

Perception

This has to do with how you view yourself as an individual. This has to do with how you see yourself overall as well as how you perceive the "physical" version of yourself. It encompasses how you view both your personal and work lives.

It also covers how you see the relationships in your personal and professional life. It also has to do with how you view your environment, your situation, and your current stage of life.

Since our perceptions of others and ourselves can occasionally be wildly inaccurate, perception is likely one of the largest sinners in our lives. It's possible that how you view yourself differs from how other people see you.

However, we all see ourselves in unique ways. We all have a certain self-perception that is influenced by our ideas as well as, to some extent, by outside influences like our upbringing and the opinions of others.

Therefore, it's critical to invest time in self-evaluation and self-acquaintance.

The development of a healthy degree of self-esteem depends on this self-awareness. You will develop self-confidence and a good, loving self-perception if you are comfortable with who and what you are.

It will be simpler for people to view you in the same light as you if you begin to see yourself as a kind, positive person. You will project to the outside world what you believe to be true of yourself.

To go even further, the perspective of your life and environment also plays a part in this. Your self-esteem is greatly influenced by what you observe in your life, how you view your surroundings, and your present state of affairs.

Your self-esteem will suffer if you are dissatisfied with your life or your surroundings. On the other hand, you will probably feel happier overall and have a higher degree of self-esteem if you approach life with positivity and thankfulness.

Since most people are already hard on themselves and take other people's judgments seriously, how other people see us also has an impact on our sense of self-worth. We readily enable this perspective to undermine our self-esteem if we believe that we are not as worthy or appealing as someone else.

The majority of people make the costly error of trying to elevate the views, remarks, and/or judgments of others. They ultimately experience emotions of inferiority and/or unworthiness. Once more, this can lead to significant declines in self-esteem as well as increased worry and/or hopelessness.

Think positively about yourself to give yourself a confidence boost!

The Significance Of Stereotyping, Growth Theories, And Errors.

Every chance is challenging for pessimists, and every opportunity is challenging for optimists.

Important new findings have been discovered in the understanding of children's desire to attempt new things and their fear of failing. This consequently has an impact on their resilience, self-worth, and confidence.

Carol Dweck 6, a psychologist, and her Colombian colleagues have collaborated for a decade.

Stanford conducted a poll with elementary school pupils, focusing on how they responded to praise. She discovered that her kids were predisposed to one of two viewpoints. In order to avoid failing, youngsters only select careers they believe are suitable for their intellect level, adhering to a "stereotype" in the process. Second, a child with a "growth mindset" is more likely to be healthy because they are open to trying new things even if they fail since they view these experiences and obstacles as chances to learn and grow.

Dweck discovered that a youngster's experience receiving admiration directly affected which child he adopted this style of thinking. Generally speaking, the first group of youngsters who had a "fear of failure" were used to hearing compliments on their intelligence, such as "smart and smart." Still, the second group was used to hearing praise for their efforts rather than their accomplishments.

"Emphasizing effort gives children a variable that they can control," says Carol Dweck. They start to believe that they have power over their achievement. Stressing natural intellect takes control away from kids and doesn't offer helpful coping mechanisms.

Stereotypes' Effect on Children

Individuals who hold stereotypes think that they are "fixed" in nature and are incapable of growing or changing over time. As a result, stereotypes have a negative impact on children's attitudes toward learning and education, as well as their openness to trying new things and challenges. It will be challenging for kids to engage in sports or academic pursuits if they don't think they can improve and grow over time. They are far more inclined to stick to what they are good at and think that their "natural" qualities exist. When they attempt something new for the first time and fail to grasp it "correctly," it is evidence of their low IQ.

Stereotyping children is highly linked to evaluation praising. This is due to the fact that they "praise" kids based on how aware they are judged to be. For instance, if we tell our kids that we are intelligent, they can feel pressured to live up to this impression and begin to shy away from answering inquiries about their intelligence out of concern that they won't measure up. As a result, individuals might grow distasteful of tests and exams in general, which might make them detest them and prevent them from ever being taught or learning anything.

As previously mentioned, a mindset is an assortment of individual beliefs that shape our actions and perspectives toward ourselves and other people. That being said, it's critical to identify variations in growth attitude.

Equally important are stereotypes, and it's crucial to avoid categorizing kids as having either one. It is important to remember that individuals seldom fall into a single category. Depending on our circumstances and emotions, every one of us exhibits unique traits in our thought processes.

Making errors as teaching moments

"It's not a failure until you start blaming others for your mistakes."- John Wood.

Children's perception of and attitude toward mistakes is another major factor contributing to stereotypes. Since mistakes are a natural part of life, children who fear making them are less likely to take on new challenges and try novel things. However, this does not prepare them well for the realities of adulthood.

It is imperative to acknowledge that the attitudes we adopt as parents significantly influence our children's ability to learn from their errors or their fear of making mistakes. It makes sense that, as parents, we would wish to shield our kids from harm, disappointment, or any mistakes. We frequently find ourselves "saving" them from trying circumstances because we love them so much that we cannot stand to watch them suffer.

Even with the best of intentions, when we meddle too much in their lives, we frequently deny our kids the chance to make errors and pick up important lessons that only experience can impart.

Young children must be given the freedom to play and take chances without feeling that their parents are judging them or correcting them.

Furthermore, by constantly alerting kids to potential dangers, we might instil in them a sense of fear for their lives. By demonstrating that we are not ready to trust them and that we do not believe they can learn from their mistakes and move on, we do not unintentionally give them more power. Sayings like "I told you" prevent kids from listening to us because they absolve us of accountability for our errors and prevent them from understanding the lessons that come with consequences.

When managed properly, childhood can provide invaluable life lessons. Sometimes, letting kids make mistakes and dealing with the fallout teaches them to make mistakes. Children will, therefore, learn to deal with their errors and become more adept at long-term mistake prevention.

We show kids that it's okay to make mistakes—both verbally and physically—by modelling growth-oriented behaviour for them. Children who receive criticism, reprimands, or expressions of sadness for their failures are more prone to internalize stereotypes. Still, as we've found, this can also have a detrimental effect on their learning style and capacity to create new technologies.

Parents must believe that their children can get over their frustration and agitation since doing so builds their resilience and confidence. We don't do them any favours when, for instance, we try to invite them to a birthday party, and they decline or ask the soccer coach to prolong the game time because we are giving our kids a great chance to strengthen their "disappointed" muscles.

Kids should understand that it's okay to fail and that feeling depressed, anxious, or angry is natural. They learn how to succeed by conquering challenges rather than by eliminating them.

Therefore, the alternative—no matter how difficult—is to observe what errors you need to force your kids to make. These mistakes are referred to as "affordable" mistakes because children may recover from the immediate and reasonable repercussions of them and find a method to do so in order to fix them in the long term, unlike "affordable" mistakes that might cause major agitation or injury.

Therefore, set an example for your kids by modelling this conduct and being willing to make mistakes. Then, out of nowhere, they appear, deciding against saving them from disappointment and frustration in favour of giving them a chance to exercise their "disappointed muscles."

Creating A Helpful Environment.

Establishing and preserving self-esteem requires a supportive environment. Your sense of self-worth and general wellbeing can be significantly enhanced by surrounding oneself with supportive people and cultivating wholesome relationships. We will go over specific steps in this chapter to assist you in creating a nurturing atmosphere that promotes self-esteem.

Step 1: Assess Your Connections

Consider your present relationships and evaluate how they affect your sense of self. Determine who encourages and supports you and who can be a bad influence. Think about the traits you look for in a helping partner.

Step 2: Establish Limits

Set sensible limits in your interpersonal interactions. Be assertive and explicit in communicating your wants, values, and boundaries. Prioritize your well-being and learn when to say no.

Step 3: Be in the company of uplifting people

Look for uplifting people in your life. Interact with people that motivate and inspire you. Make connections with like-minded individuals; they may be a great source of inspiration and encouragement.

Step 4: Foster Relationships of Support

Foster connections based on mutual respect, trust, and assistance. Encourage honest and open conversation with those you care about. Look for mentors or role models who can offer direction and inspiration.

Step 5: Look for Expert Assistance

Think about contacting life coaches, therapists, or counselors for expert assistance. They can offer unbiased perspectives, direction, and resources to assist you in enhancing your self-worth and skillfully overcoming obstacles.

Step 6: Connect with Helpful Groups

Seek out organizations or communities that share your passions, interests, or aspirations for personal growth. Participating in these groups enables you to meet people who share your interests and obtain inspiration and support.

Step 7: Accept Being Vulnerable

When you're around people you can trust, feel free to be vulnerable. Be honest about your hopes, worries, and difficulties. Genuineness and openness have the power to build stronger bonds and a nurturing atmosphere.

Step 8: Engage in Active Hearing

Learn how to listen intently to strengthen your bonds with others. Pay close attention to others and be empathetic. You contribute to a nurturing atmosphere that fosters growth for both parties when you listen and comprehend others genuinely.

Step 9: Show Appreciation

Give thanks and appreciation to the persons in your life who have been a source of support. Let them know how much you appreciate their help and presence. Gratitude builds a sense of belonging and strengthens beneficial relationships.

Step 10: Minimize Your Contact with Harmful Influences

Determine what bad influences are present in your life, such as unhealthful relationships, excessive use of social media, or negative media coverage that lowers your self-esteem. Limit the amount of time you spend with negative influences and put more of an emphasis on optimism.

Step 11: Show Up with Support

Become a helpful influence in other people's life. Encourage, sympathize with, and comprehend those around you. Supporting others fosters a mutually beneficial environment that benefits all parties.

Create a location that nurtures your self-esteem and encourages personal development by creating a friendly environment. Having a supportive network and maintaining wholesome relationships will have a big impact on your general wellbeing and sense of self. Recall that creating a supportive environment is a continuous effort, so keep an eye on things and make adjustments as necessary to keep things upbeat and cheerful.

Signs of a Positive Self-Esteem.

Learning how to recognize healthy self-esteem is crucial, in addition to realizing the advantages of boosting your confidence and self-worth. Let's examine what constitutes a good sense of self-worth.

- The antithesis of excessive or poor self-esteem: Having a balanced, constructive, and positive self-perception is essential to having healthy self-esteem. It occurs when your self-esteem isn't exaggerated. Possessing an unreasonable, extremely selfish, and borderline narcissistic perception of oneself is a sign of excessive self-esteem. This person would be someone who feels superior to everyone else and finds it difficult to listen to and be sympathetic to others. They behave entitled and believe they are flawless. They behave exquisitely and want to be given everything they want, even if it means harming other people. This kind of self-worth verges on bullying and renders you insensitive to other people. To have a healthy sense of self-worth, you must believe that you are adequate and not superior to or inferior to other people. You have the same regard and consideration for both yourself and other people.

• Capacity to communicate your needs and needs to others: A good sense of self-worth is when you can be yourself without fear of rejection or validation from other people. Individuals who have a solid sense of self-worth think that it's important to politely express their demands and feelings when it's suitable. They don't hide their emotions and act as though everything is fine. They allow themselves to be seen and heard, and they provide the same courtesy to others.

• Clear and concise boundary communication: Adolescents who possess a strong sense of self-worth invest time in getting to know who they are, what they enjoy and dislike, and how to set limits. They set limits, convey them aggressively, and warn others about the repercussions of going beyond them. They respect themselves and take themselves seriously. Others then begin to imitate and honour that pattern as well.

• Secure attachment style: Those who have a strong sense of self-worth are in several fulfilling partnerships. This is so because their interactions with people are built on an ecology of mutual respect, trust, and love. They don't think the worst of other people or themselves. They address obstacles with an attitude that demonstrates grit and belief in other people, and they have an optimistic outlook. People find them encouraging to be around because they have high self-esteem and positive views about other people. They continuously push themselves to do better and accomplish greater things because they feel the best about themselves. They definitely have a progressive mentality.

- Accept criticism with grace: Have you ever been given criticism and, despite knowing it to be accurate, found it difficult to take the advice to heart? Reason prevails when someone has a good sense of self-worth and sees mistakes and setbacks as chances to improve. They thus tend to mature more quickly and are more responsive to criticism because of this optimistic outlook. They take criticism well and use it to their advantage in a spectacular way.

Now that we know the exact formula for a strong sense of self-worth, it's time to discover how to boost your self-assurance and get rid of the negative emotions and ideas that are holding you back. One of the most effective tools you will ever have to stop failure from frequently entering your life is the ability to wear confidence. The door to the future you have always desired for yourself will be unlocked by faith. You will also be inspired to dream greater since you deserve to achieve any worthwhile objective.

Self-Care AndReflection: Rejuvenate Yourself And Grow Rich

To fully realize your potential as an empowered introvert, to keep your energy levels up, and to keep your equilibrium, self-care is crucial.

Knowing How to Look After Oneself for Thoughtful People

For introspective individuals, self-care entails creating an atmosphere of sustainability that supports your compelling needs. It means realizing the value of solitude and incorporating activities that replenish your vitality and enhance your wealth. Accept self-care as an essential component of your daily routine if you want to thrive in all facets of your life.

Putting Alone Time First

Give yourself more time to spend alone. These alone times allow you to refocus and reenergize yourself, whether you're reading, doing journalism, reflecting, or simply enjoying the silence of nature.

Creating a Calm Environment

Arrange a serene environment that complements your introverted personality. Your house should be a refuge where you can relax and think things out. Include soothing hues, soft lighting, and comfortable areas where you may unwind and find peace.

Creating Reliable Schedules

Make wise schedules that will support your mental and physical well-being. Prioritize regular sleep, wholesome meals, and physical activity. A well-maintained body and mind provide a solid foundation for accepting your independent strengths and addressing life's challenges with adaptability.

Engaging in Creative Activities

For loners, creative expression can be a powerful kind of self-care.

Use of Media Cautiously

To protect your energy and prosperity at home: Be mindful of how you use media.

Limit the amount of unpleasant or overpowering news and social media items you are exposed to.

Rather, choose media that is positive, inspiring, and consistent with your values and interests when consuming it.

Saying "no" with assurance

Find a way to channel your energy or say no to obligations that don't align with your requirements as an involved, thoughtful person. Mark your boundaries and politely turn down requests or tasks when you need to focus only on looking after yourself. By addressing your obstacles, you create room for what matters most to you.

Seeking Seclusion in the Natural World

For loners, nature may be a powerful source of rebirth. Spend time outside, immerse yourself in typical surroundings, and enjoy the tranquillity it provides.

Growing Concern

Take precautions to be focused and in the moment. You can reduce stress and become more aware of your inner needs and emotions by practising mindful breathing, introspection, or simply living in the present moment.

Developing Self-Compassion: At the forefront of your self-care journey, focus primarily on developing self-compassion. Accept that you have the right to take care of yourself and that it's acceptable to concentrate on your prosperity. Give yourself a thoughtful, tolerant indulgence, and let go of your judgment of yourself. Congratulate yourself on your efforts to maintain your inner self.

Self-care techniques can help introverts like you establish a strong foundation for well-being by implementing them into your daily routine. Accept the beauty of solitude, self-expression, and self-empathy, which will enable you to thrive and live a fulfilling life as an empowered, considerate individual.

Fundamental Principles

"People will do anything, no matter how ridiculous, to save themselves from having to face their inner selves. Enlightenment comes from making the dark aware, not from envisioning angels of light.

— Carl Gustav Jung

After some time spent posing provocative questions and grazing the surface, let's dig a little farther to get past conscious "opinions" and into subconscious "core beliefs."

Our fundamental ideas have a significant influence on both our daily choices and our abilities. The early relationships we have in life have a significant influence on how we develop our beliefs about our abilities.

Our only chance of surviving until we are able to take care of ourselves is through the relationships we have with our family, particularly the primary caregiver. Our understanding of the world, ourselves, and our role in it is shaped by the beliefs we form during this vulnerable time in life.

For small humans, even the most fundamental survival skills require a long time to learn. Most animals are able to walk immediately after birth. They immediately begin learning where to get food. In contrast, during the first six months of our lives, humans are only able to digest our mother's breast milk. It takes us another six months to learn how to walk or speak in coherent phrases. We take our sweet time, and our capacity to maintain our primary caregiver over this critical period is critical to our survival.

Due to this evolutionary characteristic of our species, from an early age, we learn to modify all of our behaviours and beliefs in order to maintain our primary caregiver's provision for us. Babies have an innate need to be pretty; in fact, research indicates that adorable babies receive greater attention from their parents (Chideya). Even though we can now walk and talk, societal acceptance demands that we "be kind to your parents" and "do what your mom says" as we get older and become children.

Every instinct in our cognitive being throughout the first one or two decades of life, including acceptability, important worries, and the desire for structure, shelter, and safety, pushes us to become the person our parents want us to be. We conform to a mould. While some of us are content in this mould and others are not, we are all sorry when we break from it.

We put ourselves in the circumstances and take acts throughout life that are dictated by our fundamental ideas about who we are, what we can and cannot do, why we are here, whether or not we deserve respect and love, and whether or not our feelings are real.

Our whole perception of the world and the roles we play are consistent with our fundamental beliefs, even though they may never come to pass. It's a self-fulfilling prophecy: our beliefs direct our emotions, which in turn direct our actions, which validates our beliefs and encourages more of the same.

Engage in Activities You Love

Engaging in activities you enjoy is one approach to cultivating a strong sense of self-worth. It might give you confidence in your abilities and self-worth. You automatically feel good about yourself and are more inclined to have a positive attitude in life when you are doing what you love. It could be anything from cooking to painting to participating in sports. The following are a few instances of things you can do to improve your self-esteem:

Engaging in regular exercise.

Having fun with loved ones and pals

volunteering or providing aid to those in need;

engaging in a passion-driven pastime or interest;

establishing and working for personal objectives.

Make time to engage in a pleasurable and fulfilling activity on a regular basis.

Get Rid of Perfectionism and Self-Criticism

Eliminating perfectionism and self-criticism is a significant step toward raising your self-esteem. It will be hard to feel good about yourself if you continuously criticize or hold yourself to unattainable standards. Rather, attempt to accomplish the following:

Begin by acknowledging that mistakes are inevitable and accepting yourself for who you are.

Avoid evaluating yourself against others. Comparing ourselves to people around us can easily lead to feelings of inadequacy, but it's crucial to keep in mind that each person is different and has both talents and faults.

Have a realistic perspective on life. It entails coming to terms with failure as a natural part of life and putting your attention on your accomplishments and advancements.

Give up whatever resentment you might be harbouring. It will be difficult to feel good about yourself if you hold grudges against people or obsess over previous slights. Rather, make an effort to forgive and let go of any bad memories.

Establish reasonable expectations and goals. It seems sense that you would feel bad about yourself if you were always establishing impossible standards for yourself. Quit placing yourself under so much stress.

Give Yourself Credit for Success

Rewarding yourself for your accomplishments, no matter how tiny, is one approach to building strong self-esteem. It could be rewarding yourself with a wonderful dinner after finishing a challenging task at work or purchasing a new book for yourself. Whatever it is, congratulations on a job well done! Pat yourself on the back!

Lastly, keep in mind that nobody is flawless, and that's alright. Although mistakes are inevitable, how you respond to them and learn from them matters. You'll be well on your way to building a strong sense of self-worth if you can learn to accept your imperfections and keep going.

Understand How To Set Limits

Setting up appropriate limits does not entail being rude or excluding others. It only entails being explicit about your needs and following through on them. You should not be afraid to speak up or to leave a situation if someone is acting beyond your boundaries. Having firm limits makes it less likely that you'll put up with bad treatment or be taken advantage of.

Saying "no" more frequently is one of the best strategies to start practising setting limits. If you tend to please people, it could be difficult to implement. It's crucial to keep in mind, though, that you owe no one your time or effort. Say "no" when someone asks you to do something you don't want to.

It is never too late to speak up or leave a situation if someone is acting outside of your bounds. Never forget that you are deserving of respect. By establishing limits and advocating for yourself, you're indicating that you won't accept anything less.

Study.com is the image source.

A Closer Examination of Fundamental Human Emotions

Emotions are famously hard to define, no doubt about it. But if there's one thing we can't dispute, it's the importance of emotions in our lives. The importance of emotion as a source of information that humans utilize to communicate and navigate the environment is sometimes underappreciated.

Of course, the study of emotions and their significance in our lives has long captivated psychologists. Truly fascinating, then, that over time, a number of theories regarding emotions and their formation have been developed.

The Theory of Evolution

According to this theory of emotion, human emotions exist because they serve an adaptive purpose. These same feelings motivate us to respond or react swiftly to the stimuli we come across, improving our chances of surviving.

It was precisely this particular skill that made it possible for both humans and animals to flourish, endure, and even procreate.

Fear motivates us to take action; we can choose to escape from our fears or meet them head-on. We look for other people's company when we fall in love, and finally, we settle down to start a family. Our ability to perceive and comprehend these feelings in both humans and animals has been essential to our long-term survival as a species.

The Theory of James-Lange

The first formal theory regarding emotions that is known to exist is the James-Lange theory. This hypothesis, which was first presented by William James and Carl Lange in 1884, is predicated on the idea that feelings are distinct from the bodily responses that our experiences cause. According to this idea, an emotion arises when a trigger initiates the body's reaction, and we feel the resulting physiological changes.

Picture Credit: emotions

The idea that our emotions preceded our physiological reactions was fundamentally challenged by the James-Lange theory. Even while this was a significant first step toward understanding human emotions beyond what is immediately apparent, there are still unanswered questions. One of the most vocal opponents of this hypothesis was the American physiologist Walter Cannon, who emphasized that physiological responses were not always or exclusively connected to certain emotions.

As an illustration, although both fear and anger raise our heart rates, they are essentially distinct feelings. Furthermore, this hypothesis fails to explain how the adrenaline that raises our heart rate only triggers certain feelings in response to certain cognitive cues.

The Theory of Cannon-Bard

Walter Cannon presented his theory since he did not agree with the James-Lange theory. Philip Bard later developed this theory, which together made up the Cannon-Bard Theory of Emotion that is still in use today. Our bodily reactions partially influence our emotional experiences. Strong physiological reactions trigger feelings like fear and anxiety, which are characterized by palpable pulses in the heart and a lurch in the stomach.

The Cannon-Bard approach, sometimes known as the Thalamic theory of emotion, explains that when we experience strong emotions and a physiological response at the same time, these may show up physically as trembling, tense muscles, or even sweating.

This is how the autonomic nervous system functions in the body and explains why we sometimes experience the fight-or-flight reaction. These autonomic reactions are to blame.

Cannon also suggested that emotional reactions occur too swiftly to be understood as byproducts of our bodily condition. Most of the time, fear is felt in a dangerous scenario before any physical symptoms appear.

The Theory of Two Factors

In relation to the previously discussed topic of adrenaline, Stanley Schacter and Jerome Singer introduced the Two-Factor Theory in 1996 in an attempt to resolve that dilemma. This theory states that feelings are the result of a series of events.

Source of Image: Slideshare.net

According to the hypothesis, physiological changes begin at the end and are then followed by cognitive attributions to the cause of the changes. Finally, there is an emotional experience at the conclusion.

By seeking to take into consideration the potential ambiguity that arises when physiological changes occur, Schacter and Singer expanded upon the James-Lange theory. According to this hypothesis, emotions are linked to modifications that are evaluated in light of the individual's surroundings and circumstances.

Putting Yourself Back Together

Codependent people frequently have a lower sense of their value, which makes them heavily dependent on other people for validation and approval. Building a strong feeling of self-worth, self-love, and self-esteem is essential to escaping the clutches of codependent tendencies. This chapter explores the critical role that self-esteem plays in the codependency recovery process and offers doable strategies for rebuilding it.

The Fundamentals of Self-Love and Self-Worth
Self-worth and self-love are fundamental components of a sound sense of self-worth. The foundation for codependency recovery is provided by these two elements, which are inextricably linked. Let's examine the fundamentals of self-love and self-worth and how to cultivate them.

1. Understanding Self-Worth: Self-worth is the intrinsic value and importance you place on yourself as a person. It represents realizing your inherent value independent of approval from others or accolades. When it comes to codependency, people frequently struggle with concerns of self-worth and turn to outside validation to help them feel validated.

2. Cultivating Self-Worth: This involves changing one's perspective. It begins with the recognition that you are valuable in and of yourself and that you are worthy of love and respect in your truest form. Negative self-beliefs must frequently be dismantled in order to make room for more empowering, positive ones.

3. The Art of Loving Oneself: Treating oneself with the same love, care, and consideration that one would give to a dear friend is the foundation of self-love. It includes accepting oneself in spite of one's shortcomings and

acknowledging one's defects. The cure to the self-criticism and self-neglect that afflict many people struggling with codependency is self-love.

Realistic Steps to Promote Self-Love and Self-Worth:

- Challenging False Beliefs: Find and address the self-defeating beliefs you have in order to start the trip. Use positive affirmations to combat any feelings of worthlessness or inadequacy that you may be harbouring. Change "I'm not good enough" to something like "I inherently possess value."

- Holding Self-Compassion in Mind: Give yourself compassion and empathy, especially when you're facing hardship or self-criticism. Channel the sympathy you would feel for a close friend in a similar circumstance by visualizing the consolation and assistance you would provide.

- Defining Personal limits: Setting up and upholding sound personal limits shows others that you appreciate and cherish yourself in addition to protecting your well-being.

- Acknowledging Achievements: No matter how big or small your accomplishments are, acknowledge and appreciate them. Acknowledge and celebrate your successes to increase your sense of self-worth.

- Making self-care a priority: Give self-care a prominent place as an example of self-love. This could mean engaging in activities that support your physical, emotional, and mental health, like working out, practising meditation, taking up a hobby, or just taking some time to unwind.

Seeking Professional Guidance: You may want to think about seeking therapy or counselling if you are having trouble with deeply rooted issues related to your self-esteem. A mental health expert can help you address the underlying issues that are causing your challenges with self-worth and work together to create a more positive self-image.

- Cultivating Gratitude: Take time to consider the good things in your life to help you develop gratitude. A change in perspective from self-reproach to self-appreciation can be facilitated by gratitude.

www.ingramcontent.com/pod-product-compliance
Lightning Source LLC
Chambersburg PA
CBHW052150110526
44591CB00012B/1925